Communion Wine
in a Shot Glass

by

Morgan Nikola-Wren

Also by Morgan Nikola-Wren

Magic with Skin On, (Luminarium Press, 2017)
My Dearest Hurricane (Luminarium Press, 2017)

communion wine

——————— IN A ———————

shot glass

MORGAN NIKOLA-WREN

Luminarium
PRESS

Communion Wine in a Shot Glass

Copyright © 2018 by Morgan Nikola-Wren

All rights reserved.

ISBN: 978-0-9985898-2-4

Edited by Charity Samoulides

To Danny,
who always makes me feel safe
and challenged at the same time.

And to Chris,
for what, I feel, are obvious reasons.

TABLE OF CONTENTS

o n e

t w o

TABLE OF CONTENTS

TABLE OF CONTENTS

f o u r

f i v e

TABLE OF CONTENTS

communion wine

────────── IN A ──────────

shot glass

Don't try to sell me a god
who will pull me out of my grief,
kicking and caked with despair.

Give me One who will dive
down its throat with me.

one

The Book of More, I

Write about more.

Write about the fears that
keep swarming around your head
'til they've clustered themselves into
a rotten, rusted halo.

Write about how you answered
to the name "not good enough"
so many times you want
to cut your tongue in two.

Write about how you slammed
your fists into the question,
"am I getting it right"
over and over
'til you could write
prophecies of your own downfall
across the wall with the blood
that spilled from your knuckles.

Write about how,
on your darkest days,
you keep a collection of
all the things you've never found
growing inside of you,
splayed desperately
across your stone heart
as if it were an altar.

The Book of "Let's Get Something Straight"

I'm no saint.
I'm just pretending to be
the best version of myself.

I've got
the kind of demons
who always seem to know
where I am.

I've got
one of those spirits
that's a patchwork of
all the people
I planned to become.

I'm the sort of woman
who looks nothing like her poetry
or her prayers.

The Book of Punching Myself in the Teeth with My Own Prayers

You cheap, church-white bones,
picked clean of any life and pretending
to breathe out truth.

You passion(less) play
at confession.
You never color your words
outside of lines that you scripted for
polite dinner conversation.
You dress yourself in something like
sanitized; set fire to every honest word
you keep concealed in
the folds of your clothing
'til you find yourself naked but
never revealing anything,
just smearing the ashes of your story
across your forehead.

You red-hot rage, climbing
the chimney you've
made of your throat.

You dizzy inferno,
you don't even know
what it is that you're trying
to smoke out of your chest.
All you can remember is
the hurt you keep cradled in there.

You mouth like a furnace
of fiery tongues,
you answer to every name
but "enough."

You savage slap to any gospel sprouting
in your mouth.
You spit teeth like seeds into
the soil path beneath your feet.

You run your faith into the ground and
hope any words like what you needed
will grow on your tongue,
despite the thorns in your throat
and the stones in your stomach.

11

And you're praying all-the-while
that the passersby will get
the grace you keep
talking yourself out of.

The Book of Not Enough

I can't stop
cramming my life
full to the brim
with too little.

The Book of the
Salvation Complex

Knowing You exist
was never the problem. In fact,
it's this very faith that lights
hellfire up my dreams
almost every night.

It's believing You love me
that is asking for a miracle.

You cannot tell me often enough
that I am safe. Or maybe
You've said it too many times.
Maybe this whole house I've
made of my body
is painted the color
of Your mercy 'til it all
looks the same to me. 'Til I can't
recognize myself as something
worth dying for anymore.

So until I can kill
this self-loathing inside of me,
and feel Your salvation
flowing through me like
a newly loosed spirit,
I will just have to trust You
to love me for
all the conviction
that I have yet to nail
to my tongue.

The Book of
"Be Still and Know"

I want to be the woman
who wraps her fists in
angel wings and faces
down the underworld
with fight flying from
her hands
and lightning charging down
her arms.

I want to hold back hate
with thunder in my throat.

I want to kiss all the decay
from everyone who's ever
placed the feeling of home,
soft and glowing
in my chest.

But right now,
I'm just trying to untangle
myself from this sorrow.

Right now,
I'm just asking for
the strength to spill out of myself
in a sea of tears,
and for friends that will
walk across it to find me.

Right now, I just need You
to increase the distance between
a prayer and a panic attack.

Right now, I just need You
to steady my hands
long enough
for me to lay my heart
against the cosmic longing
of Your fingers.

The Book of Unbelief*

Your embrace is a miracle,
by which I mean
it is the sort of marvel I can
run into and
rip my way out of
all at once.

You're the kind of truth that burns
so wondrous-bright,
every part but the deep of me
doesn't believe it.

Still, I find You
strung like lanterns
across these renegade heartstrings
that reach out of my chest
and far into forever.

* "*Lord, I believe; help my unbelief!*" –Matthew 9:24b, New
International Version

18

The Book of This
Body of Death*

I reach through my prayers
and come out
with heaven on my hands,
yet everything I touch
seems to end up dirty.

My gut
is a coiled gargoyle crouching
ever wise, ever watchful
in the pit of my stomach.

But a demon dressed
like good intentions
always finds itself sticking
to my lips.

*"For I do not understand my own actions. For I do not do
what I want, but I do the very thing I hate ... Wretched man that
I am! Who will deliver me from this body of death?" –Romans
7:15, 24 English Standard Version

The Book of Doubt

I am alone here.

A temple floor kisses
my bare feet, and they
are awash
in the feel of frigid marble,
as though Your presence has
poured cool water over them.

I want so badly
to see You before me.
But my shame will not allow it.
It is too busy searching my soul for
something to give back to You.

(As if the sum total of all my lack
could somehow balance this out.)

I am weighing
the vastness of Your sacrifice
against the blind faith in my hands when
You tip
the scales* in my eyes,
and I see there
is no offering as precious
as this honest doubt
that's unfurling just for You.

*In the Book of Acts, Chapter 9, the apostle, Paul, is healed of
his blindness when something like scales fall from his eyes.
Also, a reference to "tipping scales in someone's favor" when
they deserve less. Behold. Wordplay.

The Book of Believing*

I believe
just enough to pray,
"God keep me believing
for one more day."

*A friend of mine once said "Faith itself is a gift—one I have to
ask God for daily." That has stuck with me more than a
hundred tips or platitudes on how to banish the doubt and/or
questions.

22

The Book of *Lady Lazarus

I keep making beds
in burial grounds,
like I've got a body bag for skin.

Tonight, I'm just
a collection of unholy ghosts
shaped like a girl.

I have tasted
all the women I could have been
dying behind my lips
before any of them could
find my voice.

So many of them have
fallen silent down my throat,
that I keep an underworld
tucked beneath my tongue
and have long since grown tombstones
for teeth.

So if You've got
another resurrection in You,
I could sure use it now.

*The phrase "Lady Lazarus" is taken from the title of
a poem by Sylvia Plath.*

24

The Book of "Why Stay?"

Because there is a beauty
shivering right through my skin
and into a place buried
deeper than bones.

Because there is a Voice
trickling through all the times I
felt Truth spill my soul out
of all this hopelessness and into
a place so much softer.

Because that Voice
calls out a name I have
never before heard but know is my own,
and it promises me I can take
this faith further than my fears.

t w o

The Book of More, II

Write about more.

Write the prayers that are
too shy, too sacred
to spread themselves
between polite company like
a tablecloth.

Write about how
your voice goes soft when
it sits down to dinners.
How you drape your life story in
a dove-wing white that flutters like a
satin slip, skirting around all the words
you want to taste.

Write about how you
take an emery board to your humor,
lacquer a pale pink bubble
over your laugh--never too angry,
you scrub the piss from your stories and
strain the vinegar from your smile.

Write about how you hang
a halo on your conversation
'til you
just talk in circles each night.

Write all that inconvenient talk your
tongue tucks neatly
into your cheek,
as if putting all your questions to bed,
telling them
there's nothing to fear,
nothing to fight,
not knowing they've already made such
a tangled monster
out of you.

The Book of Not Quite

I just want graceful prayers
laid lovely across my tongue
like the Eucharist.

But I am not quite praise like a Sunday
morning service, spreading languid
gold across everyone's faces.
I'm (just) the jokes crouching in
hymnal margins, hasty scribbles
balled up and pinching your mouths into
disapproval.

Still I swear I've got
prayer sleeping in every
word I say.
Even the sounds that
cut savage through my teeth
and make the minutes bleed
so slow and pained past us
are asking Love
to curl up in the cracks of me.

The Book of "Just a Guess"

I think my soul tastes
something like communion wine
in a shot glass.

The Book of Guilt

My God,
You keep begging me
to come off this cross of mine,
but I haven't quite mastered how
to accept your embrace
without nailing my arms open.

Maybe that's why every time I try
to hand my life over to You,
it slips right through my palms,
as if holes had been
hammered into them.

The Book of Shame

I dare you to believe
that I fell straight
from God's fingers
'cause, well,
one of us has to.

For now, all I know
is that my back
is a broken parable,
and it's hinging, hanging
my head to the ground,
'cause I can't get this story straight.

My spine is a constant
question mark curl,
asking why I could never
believe the fable of the father
running with arms thrown open
to meet his sin-scarred son*

I say that it all
seemed more fairytale than fact,
even when the story was
tripping right from God's lips
flying fast as it could get to me
and asking
to be wrapped in my trust.

*Reference to the parable of The Prodigal Son, found in the gospels of Matthew and Luke.

The Book of the 2016 Election

Yesterday, the country
collapsed in on itself, only to sift through
the wreckage and find
what it was made of all along.

Today, what passes for patriotism
ripped a boy's face open, stripes
of red blood flagging him
as unwelcome
'til he could not recognize
his own despair staring
back at him from the news.*

Tonight, a street not so far away
is speaking in gunshots.
And people I have never met
are telling me to stay in this coffee house
'til something other than a firearm
can light my way home.

Tonight, some strangers and I sit
at an oversized oak table where
we patch together our pain
like a makeshift quilt.

Tonight, America is a gun pointed
to the heavens like a broken prayer,
shooting the stars right out of our eyes.

Tonight, we are fighting like everything
we want to say is hidden in our fists.

And I wonder if the world is so hell-bent
on ripping the kindness right out of us
because it never learned to ask
for what it needed.

So God, grant me a ruthless softness,
the kind that never leaves my touch, no
matter how many people come at me
with their tongues steeped in hate
and their fingers steeple-sharp with
something I never want to confuse for
You again.

The Book of Misshapen Mouthpieces

I wish I never knew
the sound of screaming
trying to pass
for scripture.

I wish I could simply
read the Bible and not see rage
storming across the pages.

Now the clouds are crying
all the tears I am afraid to,
and this city slides its way across
the rain slick windows of my car
as I tear off to
somewhere softer, truer, than this.

I wonder if I'll ever find it.

I demand to know why
You never show up,
not any more.

And when the lightning
forks five ways,
I insist that I'm insane
for seeing a hand
reaching out to me,
for hearing how the thunder cracks
like a sob breaking in the back
of a universe-sized throat.

The Book of the Inevitable

Tonight, my prayers smell
like the sky before a storm.

The Book of "It's Not Like He Doesn't Know I'm Mad."

My God,
my poems
seem to like You
often enough.

I'm just not sure about
the rest of me
sometimes.

Sometimes
the absolute
best I can manage
is wanting
to want
the right thing.

Sometimes,
it's a miracle I
speak to You at all,
my tongue having been
drained dry from crying
Mercy!
for so many nights.

But I manage.
I write out my grievances.
I hold tight to my pen, and drag it
through Your name,
over and over, until my hands,
become a prayer-shaped fist,
and I hope You're up
for the fight,
'cause tonight,
I want to know
why You (we?) always
let ignorance borrow
Your voice,
let hate steal
Your face.

I want You to tell me
why You don't come down and
rip the holy off the hands
that bludgeon others
in Your name.

The Book of "Haven't We Had Enough?"

My God,
I ache for a day when we learn
to stop speaking militia,
when we smile at one another
and our beliefs don't line up like
soldiers across our lips.

My God,
teach us to stop
embedding bullets in our words.
Or, at least, tell me
why fear always travels in fists,
why we dress
a touch as healing as Yours
in brass knuckles,
why the truth sits like a blade
between our teeth.

My God,
there are voices I wish
would stop wearing Your words.
And they keep tying
tears to my breath
'till I'm choking on Your gospel
'til I've got no choice
but to reach down into myself.
I pull my hand from my throat,
clenching something tight
inside of it.
(I never knew
how much my mouth
was shaped like a first
before now.)

Now,
I smear all this filth across
my palms like an ill-conceived fortune,
like I never thought to look
anywhere but my own hands
for a hint of You.

44

The Book of Bad Theology

There are churches I
swagger into like they are
the bar fight I have always wanted.

And my tongue curls tight
around the broken bottle I
have made of my theology.

I know.

I'm working on it.

The Book of Saint Fearsome

There was once (more than once)
a girl with a crippled tongue that
couldn't stop bleeding
all the wrong prayers,

and she called herself Saint Fearsome:
a walking, two-fisted church,
who was a bit more fight
than a faith should be,
all pressed into a pair
of sobbing lungs
pushing out wet prayers to
a God so big, He could cry
even harder than she could.

The Book of
the Long-Overdue Apology

On behalf of Christians everywhere,
I am sorry.

I am sorry
you know the terror of
staring down the barrel
of a sawed-off scripture
held in hands that have
no intention of
shaping themselves into
something like repentance.

I am sorry
these little lights of ours*
have blinded us to your pain.

I am sorry
for all the times we've seen
for ourselves the way suffering spills out
of you and did nothing
to stop up the wound, because nothing
felt like enough.

And I am so, so sorry
for the way we
have whittled God down
into a pocket-sized privilege,
made Him small enough
to slip into our pockets when we
needed a V.I.P. badge.
It's no surprise we
can't remember
where we put Him now,
when we need Him the most.

*Reference to the children's song, This Little Light of Mine,
written by Harry Dixon Loes, circa 1920.*

The Book of Unlearning

God, give me
that terrifying blessing
of unlearning.

That feel of
tendons untangling from
the worldview they've been woven into.

That sound of
a symphony
un-layering itself until I
can tiptoe across
the tremor of it all,
my feet whispering against
a path of naked notes lined
up against each other like
a new backbone.

And oh, it frightens me to say it,
but I do not wish to be unwavering.

I want
to pull this faith of mine
out of me by the roots,
tears kissing it like dewdrops.

I want
to undress it in the soft glow
of a bedside lamp
and place
all its earnest, tired trembling
in Your hands.

The Book of What I Want

When I finally come to
what might be a confession,
with questions knotted through my brow,
and transgressions trembling naked
on my lips,
my knees knocking, clinging
to each other like they learned
never to trust anyone else…

When I hobble my way into
something like safety,
somewhere that feels halfway holy,
I am not wishing to walk into a sermon.
I don't want to be lectured.
I don't want to be shamed.
Or fought.
Or fixed.
Or hidden.
Or humored.

I just want to be healed.

So, tell me I'm worth
the time that takes.
But only if you mean it.

The Book of One Day

I can feel my whole head shaking
with the weight of my words,
my tongue sweating beneath
all the stories I am afraid
to spit out.

And I'm praying God gives me
friends who can wear doubt like
a familiar embrace.

Give me
a faith that unfurls itself
into so much more than I've
been taught to expect.

Give me
a revolution small enough to
fit in my rib cage,

something tailor-made
to the size of my hands,

something I
can carry out church doors
and dip into the streets that stream
beneath my feet,

something I
can keep safe as a flask against me,

something I
can pour into people's sight,

something I
can smear across a time-worn stage,

something that
can turn a cabaret into a confessional.

God, split me
red-curtain open
when I find the right eyes.

three

The Book of More, III

Write about more.

Write about trying
to fit your womanhood into
words that you once looked for
in sermons that seemed to have
no use for a voice like yours.

Write about all the times
you cut off your tongue so you
wouldn't take up too much space
in your own mouth.

Write about how you swallowed your
pride, subdued your passion,
but still always managed to come out the
wrong kind of woman with no rights to
any position that was too high, any
purpose that was too loud, any prayer
that sounded too much like power.

Write about the first time
a professor told you that being
wrenched from Adam's ribs
did not make you any less Deity,
it just meant that God had
scooped all the feminine
from their initial image
just to slip it into your skin.

Write about how
this beautiful heresy hung like
a chandelier between your ears,
painting the scriptures
in a new light,
as though you were just
introducing them to your eyes.

Write about all the times God
told men to be meek and gentle.

Write about all the times God
compares Himself to a Mother.

Write about all the times you
almost deleted this poem.

The Book of the Sunday Dress

Lord, sometimes,
just the thought of You
sends my eyes swimming
in holy water tears
and sinks something I still
can't name
down into the marrow of me, while I
pulse electric with a
storm of rituals I have crafted
especially for us.

But today,
I am pinched into one of those
starched Sunday dresses.

The kind that closes
tight around my shoulders
like a pair of hands keeping me
in my place.

The kind with a high collar
that chokes the truth
back down my throat.

The kind with skirts full as a birdcage, so
the wings on my heels keep slamming
into all this lace and satin like
blind angels.

This is all just another way of saying this
power that has
long since sprouted from my skin,
keeps getting smothered by
all this delicate, so tear the timidity from
my voice and
rattle my words free
of all this liturgy.

Set a song loose in my bones tonight.
They have been begging to dance
for far too long.

The Book of the "Weaker Sex"

I am still learning
to celebrate this
skin of mine.

.

The Book of the White Male Nationalists

This screaming?
It's simple.
It's softness.
Right there.
In the breakable
snail shell curl of your fists

Anger is such a fragile,
lace-clear thing after all.
Veiling your face like a bride,
but we can all see
the fury for ourselves,
the way it pins mouths
wide and red as blooming roses on all of
your faces, the rage rouging your
sharpened cheeks as you sail down
church aisles, a fleet
of combat-boot clad feet
stomping across a ground that is
so sacred to me, and blessing hands that
bruise young girls' memories
all the while.

You marry your eyes
to the color of catastrophe
'til you can
find disaster anywhere but
the places you don't want to.
Fear is such a fumbling-blind thing
after all. It gives you
the kind of opinion
that sets up house
at the top of your lungs,
but there's a world
of difference between
making noise
and making sense.

And I make myself
remember all the times I
made hate look an awful lot
like holiness.

And I make myself
pray for you.

Some nights,
I am not up to the task.

But other days, I hope
whatever kindness it was that never
cradled your words,
whatever love it was that that never
drug the demons
from your doctrine,
comes to you, cracks you open,
shatters you into a heap
of small mercies,
finds you in a faith that makes room
for your inadequacies.

And one day, I'll pray you find
that it was never about
being superior to begin with.
Find forgiveness
before it's too late.

The Book of the Adam's Apple

You brave little boast in
your own weakness.

You tremble frightened with every
scream they
set loose on us.

You always shake like a fist when
shouts fight against our power.

You knock at the necks
of these men, your masters
to get our attention,

and you tell us
there is nothing original
about the way they pin sin
on the softness of our flesh,
as though forbidden fruit never built
a home in their own throats.

The (First) Book of the Dead*

If you ask me
why the blush has been
drained from my cheeks,

if you tell me
I should be ashamed of all
the people I had to become
before I believed I could
ever get this right,
before I found that this faith
reached past my ability to
feel perfection in my grasp,

if you're indignant that the guilt
has gone out of my voice,

I will, by the grace of God,
bite back all curses begging
to be let off my tongue—
begging 'til they burst, a sour juice
swishing through my cheeks.

67

Then, I will send you a smile,
stitched shut, as with old needlework.

See, I used to
slice off the inconvenient
from my life's journey.
Offer it to the underside
of the nearest rug,
like a tithe to the story I
felt I owed you.
As if that were any different
than pulling my body so wide open
that I tore myself to pieces
for the boys who
borrowed God's name.
Neither of you wanted
all of me.

So how dare you say my
bad days should be
any place other
than sewn through the seams
of my coats? They hold me
together like the rest of my story,
and heaven knows I needed them.

Some nights my mistakes
were my most steadfast friends.
Now, my pockets are
heavy and haunted
with the ghosts of all the girls I
used to be.

I do not mind
carrying them through
the life that outlived them.

I love telling them yes
when they ask
if the years grow any kinder.
I just wish I didn't have
to answer for them so often,
as if the way they laid themselves
down gasping by
the side of the road
did not speak for itself.

*Almost titled, "To All the People who Think I Don't Sound
Remorseful Enough when I Talk about Where I've Been."*

The (Second) Book of the Dead

I give thanks for
the women I have been before.
For the pure sacrifice they
made of themselves.
The way they passed my body
one to another,
put themselves to death beneath
the weight of wanting something more,
rather than to drag me through their
worlds again and again.

Now, they make a mausoleum
of the desert road that stretches
behind my heels
while a warm wind
takes your hand and hurries you
past them on hushed steps.

-

Half-buried in a by-way and choking up
gravel lays a girl who felt her voice
turn to pebbles in her mouth
when she learned that God did not
want women with a will like hers.
If you look closely,
you can still see
her fighting all the strength in her throat.

-

Not far from her,
a gangly creature with
pencils for legs is
spread across the highway, swallowing
her protests when she is told that her
flesh should be a spotless sacrifice to a
husband who might one day
see her as sullied,
should she ever forget that she
is guarding the gate of her worth against
every young man's wanting.

(As if manliness was next to godliness,
but for all their holy power, they could
not hold back the groping from their
hands.)

And I'm sure it was something
well-meaning that placed
all this responsibility on her,
as if crowning her shoulders
with it, but the weight
of all this desire
hunches her head to the ground,
and her dignity melts into maggots filling
her stomach, as if she really has gone
rotten, a rose plucked apart
piece by piece, with each pair
of wandering hands
'til there is nothing left in her
that is worth wanting.

-

A few years down the Fastlane,
a young woman crumbles herself into a
roadside attraction.
She is clouded in the rotten-sweet
smell of sweat-soaked clothes
wilting at her feet.
She is a riot reeking of a lifetime-full
of empty expectation
and no one to listen to her heart
burst open like the bloated carcass of
whatever it was that died inside of her.

She remembers hearing
how no woman would
open her legs for any reason other than to
trap love in between them,
and the sun sets fire to the hollow laugh
that is propping
her mouth open.

She spits out all the nonsense
assumptions that have been spooned into
her mouth from such a young age. Love
(or something like it) is the naked
declarations she left sleeping in her
basement without saying goodbye.
Without even looking back.
What she's chasing
is the racing
of her heart as she slides
into a fast-moving car.
She just wants to feel something.
Or she wants to forget.

-

Just a few epiphanies ahead of her,
another girl is hemorrhaging confessions.

She tries
to tell a boy—who is having gin for
breakfast—that she wants
to stop prying herself apart.
She is tried of trying
to fit the pieces of her into experiences
made too small for what she is really
searching for.

She sees now that it
was never about
a man watching her from
some future others wished for her,
thinking she looked best with
her virtue dressed in white lace.

It was about her.

And she is tired
of wrapping wayward spirits in
the deep of her, trying to see
what it is like to hold onto something,
only to rip it out again.
She cannot bring in
the Purpose that calls
on the wind every night
if she keeps making a
barbed wire fence of her rib cage.

And the boy with the gin laughs.
In her face. For a long time.
As if taking yourself back
from your decisions,
from the roles chosen for you
since childhood,
from the boys who never
got deeper than your bare skin,
sounds an awful lot like impossible.

I look back at her.
Watch pain pick
at the corners of her eyes
like flies.
And I hope she hears me
when I tell her the tears are better spent
so many other places.

-

I look forward and wonder
who I will hand this flesh off to
when the time catches up to me.

The Book of Rebirth

When I swaddle my faith
so tightly that I smother it,
feel it fall silent in my arms…

When despair slides cold as
death down my throat…

When all the fight goes stillborn
inside my mouth…

When my words go empty as
an abandoned school…

Something frantic in me dares scream
that I am not done yet, so I
dig my fingers into the belly
of the beast I have become.

I carve at the cavern I
have made of my chest,
hollow of all breath,
'til my hands come up
painted scarlet
with the brave and blood-soaked
truth of me.

I string them across a gasp,
a death rattle trembling in my palms.

I fling them up to the sky
like an umbilical cord
to a God that knows the honor
of draping the word "mother"
over His name.

I tell Him this world
is a hell of a story,
but I suspect I will not
make it out alive,
so when my body breaks
like bread beneath me,
I pray He pulls
the string of every sound I
spilled up to Him,
hauls me past the clouds so I
can feel his face between my hands
spread wide as galaxies,
and my heart a cosmic expanse
just learning how
to fit into a fraction
of whatever my Maker is made of.

The Book of the Madonna/Whore Complex

Some days,
I make tightropes
out of telephone wires.

Some days,
I'm pinned to the ground
under the weight
of my wings.

Turns out I'm not the saint
I so wanted to be.
Just an abstinent whore
with a hunger for prayers.

Still, I'm not the demon
I worried I was.
Just an angel who can fit
more curses in her mouth
than most.

The Book of Celebration

I found God buried in
the so-called sinful of my silhouette.

I finally dug faith out of
the generous curve of my hip, so I
plant love in the soft arches of my feet
and send them off to
somewhere like a celebration.

I am coming
to terms
with the dove-soft of my arms.

I am learning
to carry
the sacred swell of my breasts
with pride.

I am walking
in time
to the prayer between my legs.

And a blood-red smile smears
like a scarlet hallelujah
across my lips.

The (First) Book of Undoing

Unlace my lungs
into something slow and easy again.

Something big enough to fit
all the words that frighten me.

Right now, I'm just all
the things I never say,
trapped in quick snatches of breath.

Make me more.

Make me better.

The (Second) Book of Undoing

On second thought "better"
is a tired, stale demand,
clouding every room in me
with recycled, exhausted air,
planting mold in my joints,
growing rust in my eyes.

Make me new instead

four

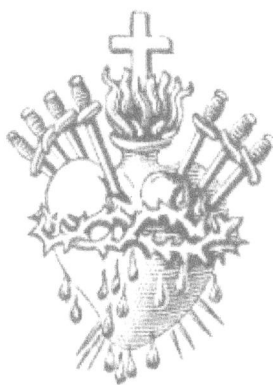

The Book of More, IV

Write about more.

Write about how faith
always seems to find you when
you stop trying
to lacquer your life over
with white paint.

Write about how it
prefers you pull
yourself apart instead,
your skin stretched across
a lifetime of coming up short,
so there is nothing left to hide.

Write about how heaven
is always gripping your hands
and hell
won't let go of your heels.

Write how the two pull so hard you find
yourself ever-stretched between paradise
and perdition, your skin so tight,
so taught,
so thin
that everyone can see
right through you.

The Book of Duality

I am the priest
and the poison,

a deity
and a demon,

the exorcism
and the entry wound by which
so much hurt can sink into me,
which is me trying to tell you
that I am dying
to pull me out of myself
and into the arms of
whatever brighter thing
I have become.

The Book of Potential

Nothing frightens me more
than all the miracles I could make
of myself.

*My preacher said "Die with failure before you die with
potential," and it's been haunting me ever since.*

The Book of "What Now?"

My feet have not met
a path that looks like You
in far too long.

Meaning I
have nothing to stand on.

And I cannot tell
if I have fallen from grace
or if You are simply
laying the ground
against my cheek, so I

can hear the pulsing
of a long since buried heart
beneath the soil, so I

can know the difference
between dead and simply digging
my way through myself, so I

can scrape away all
the inessential 'til I

sit mustard-seed small
in the palm of my hand,

ready to make myself
into something You
can make sanctified.

Ready to grow once and for all.

The Book of Sacred Sinners

I am such a soft wickedness.
Half sanctuary, half sin.

My soul is the kind
that would skinny dip
in a baptistry.

A smirk stitched to my face
like it's the only piece
of clothing I own,
like I never wanted
to press all things sacred
against the secrets of me.
The slices of me that I slip
into shame and shadow.
The back alley basilica I've
made of my body.

I have always felt
like something between
a church and a storm drain.

What I'm trying to say
is that filth always knew
just how to fall into me--maybe
that's what makes
this war inside me
so holy, the way
other people's silt
slides easy as honesty
into my arms.

The way the crook of my arm
folds like a gutter,
how it can always collect
the tears of others.
Enough to baptize anyone in.

The Book of the Fire Walker*

I used to walk through life
on legs thin as clove cigarettes.

My feet kissed danger's
coal-hot lips as I
scampered off to the next sin.

Despite having matchstick fingers,
I seemed to always leave
smoke in my wake without
ever really starting a fire.

It's why I never look
like someone who's walked through hell.

Why my words never go
saint-like and somber,
as though I taste sulfur in them.

I laugh too much to come off as refined.
A spark smolders
in my eyes as I take refuge
in retelling stories that
grew bored of me years ago.
They are familiar
though ill-fitting,
snug against all my growing, but
somewhat safe, and I
do not know what I
will find myself to be when I
step out of them.

So, I turn all the words I
want to say into a fire escape
from which to watch
myself struggle through
this conversation.

Almost titled, "How I Can Run into People I Haven't Seen in Almost a Decade and They'll Still Want to Talk about That Party House in which I Lived."

The Book of Confession

God, pour Your eyes like gold
through the slums of me.

Light me
into something
known and beautiful.

Make me
the most courageous
collection of flaws I know.

Kiss my knuckles clean
when the fight has left my fists,
and taste everything I've
pummeled my way through
day after day
to find You.

The Book of the Busy Samaritan

My God, You are
a most cosmic kind
of shape-shifter.

I shake out
the contents of my morning
across my bed in a frantic search.
I tell you I'm finding
no prayers in it,
then fly out the door
and round the corner.
So, You turn
Yourself into
the street-ridden man
with sore-spangled skin,
the one who settles for
talking to himself
because I refuse to.

I'm too busy
chasing the sound of
a cause I can manage;
it's calling to for me from
somewhere safer than this.

The Book of Renegade Prayers

My words--my prayers--are
wicked little thieves,
running from my mouth with
more conviction than they
can carry.

The Book of No Words

My God, You are
the faraway touch of a language I
have never spoke but am
desperate to remember, pressing
ever-hopeful against my tongue.

Some feelings, some facts,
will always make their homes
on the edge of my awareness.
They will tickle my voice
right on the word I can never reach.

My God, there is a desert between
my mind and my mouth,
a place where all my words
dry up.

So please, pull the prayers
from my veins before my mouth
has a chance to mangle them.

My God of unrealized genius.

My God of all places
out of words' reach.

There are some days I swear
heaven is a library
of unpublished masterpieces
and that somewhere, there's
a patron saint of songs that were
buried so deep in people's souls,
no music could ever find them.

The Book of Finally

I thought perhaps the parables
were right, that I just might have
a miracle in me.

So, I raised my secrets
from under the floorboards
and it felt
like air let loose into lungs
that thought they were done
with living.

It all happened during
the last supper I had
with women whose home
smelled like warm bread and trust.

We cut confessions open
with our teeth and
washed them down with wine.

And all the while, we sang
"blessed be the scripture you
find under bloodied fingernails,
the gospel dusted in grit
and the name of the God
who will fold Himself
small enough to fit in your arms,
so you
can feel His flay-scarred back
tremble beneath your hands
when your grief comes pouring
out of His eyes."

The Book of Still to Come

God, have faith in the fool
I have yet to become;
see the masterpieces in the messes
I will make of myself.

The Book of Morning

I love how the dawn
asks us to call it daybreak.
As if the sun has set out
to remind us just how often
newness comes on the heels
of being shattered.

It sticks like dewdrops
to destruction

So, when the day hangs heavy
as a sack of bullets in my chest,
when my throat goes dry
as a cracked soul,
when the night tastes
like tears in my mouth, I will
use it to water
seeds of tender on my tongue,
'til kindness can't help
but bloom from my lips,
gentle and sweet as
the first time I uttered it.

The Book of Deeds

I read that faith without deeds
is dead.

And I'm sure the words
were less dirge than dirt asking
to come under my fingernails,
an invitation
to plant life in my palms, but I
could never shake the fear
of rigor mortis from my fingers.

So sometimes I slip
every grand work I can find
onto my hands like jewels.

Simply put, I just want to lose myself in
some philanthropic movement, and when
I find the bitch again, she had better be
angelic.

But that is not the way it works.
Not for me at least.

See, I always change slowly
the way a story does when passed
from one tongue to another.

And deep in
the desperate need of me,
I just want to be still enough to feel
peace like a river* of
blood running through my veins,

calm enough to hear
my bones stretching across
the limits of my skin,

quiet enough to listen
to this life when it tells me
it's growing too small for whatever it is
that's taking root inside of me.

* *"A reference to the song "Peace like a River," a
spiritual sung circa the 1800s by the slaves captured
and brought from Africa to America.*

The Book of What I Really Want

In my opinion, the best poems
are just naked prayers
of some kind or another.

five

The Book of More, V

Write about more.

Write about how you want
to believe more and know less.

Write about praying
with your head pressed
to your husband's chest
after he has gone to sleep
and thinking
how God's heart sounded
exactly like that when
He slipped into skin.

Write about spending nights alone
and feeling the silence
go God-shaped around you.

Write about how your body
hums hyper-aware of every moment that
passed you down to this place.

Write about how you feel
so impossibly small inside
that vastness,
but bigger than the hundred lives
you would live if you managed
to inhale centuries.

Write about the stirring,
wordless prayers
that shake deep inside the
sacred corners of you.

Write about how this whole book
feels like a joke.

As if you could really
write about any of these things,
and profess to understand them.

As if every prayer that
passes through you
does not bring half of another
that has waited thousands of years
for you to find it.

As if there were not
ancients under your skin,
hiding you deeper and deeper
within yourself.

The Book of Color

Simply put,
I am trying to pray
in Monet's Garden.

No, really.
The ground is choking on
all this beauty, while my eyes set out
to swallow all that they can.

My words are awash
with every color they know,
but they still sound
like a blind man searching for
a rainbow in his fingertips.

I so badly want
a shrine for a mouth,
my lips a perfect fit
for all this wonder,
but nothing comes.

Instead, I love You like the poem
I'll spend my life trying to write.

The Book of Silence

On the nights
when my prayers,
my soul,
my spirit
crumble on my tongue, I lean into a gust
of wind shaped like Your embrace.

This is me trying to tell You
that I just want my name
to become another word for
the center of Your embrace.

This is my trying to tell You
that I don't want to call
Your arms by any name other
than Home.

The Book of Why I'm Still Here

It's worth it for
moments like these,
when the world goes beautiful
as a symphony wrapped around me;
when my heart hears a gospel
sung in scripture that knows
how to be something other
than a snare.

It's worth it for when I
can throw my arms open,
go racing fearlessly and whole
into all this holy,
running my fingers through
the times You taught me
all new words for repentance,
and I didn't hear shame
humming in my ears.

It's worth it for all the times You
named me reborn.

It's worth it for all the times
my tongue stumbled
over my mistakes and I
didn't feel Failure sink
its fingers into me hard enough
to leave marks.

It's worth it for the nights
when Not Good Enough
doesn't follow me home.

And it's worth it for the way
You ask
if I like how the moonlight
melts over my skin.

The Book of Grace

When I realized how much the truth
tasted like honey on my tongue,
I had to fight
not to hate every hand that smacked
confession out of people
until their teeth rattled and their
sins snaked out from their trembling lips.

It is still so hard.

Right now, I want to go to war.
To bury my teeth in the throats
of all that is wrong in this world.

But I remember all the brokenness
that began in righteous bloodshed.

I think of all the times we
have turned people into pulpits,
as though planting our feet
on others' necks
makes us stand any taller.

So instead, I hang a hallelujah
in the back of my throat
like a banner
and invite us all
to make victories of ourselves
instead of breaking others down into
battlefields.

The Book of Kindness

My God, I want to find You
in the softness that threatens
to break me,
to dip my touch in kindness,
even when it feels so useless,
even when my hands
are swearing they'll never see
another person's skin.

Make my eyes the kind
that will write prayers over
every inch of the world's wounds,
'til pain finally realizes how it feels
when someone doesn't look away.

The Book of "Prove It"

There are people who
wonder what became of my words,
wonder why my beliefs do not wear such
bright colors as before.

When I was a child, grown-ups
marveled at how I could
fit a whole rolodex
of syrupy-prim tongues
behind my teeth.

When I was a child,
I spoke like a child*.
Quick fixes always dripping from my
chin like low-hanging fruit.
My mouth unhinged,
open ever-wide, in hopes
that God would fall out eventually
so I could prove I had Him in me
the whole time.

I'm not saying I never
glimpsed Glory back then.

I'm just saying this was before
I grew uncomfortable
with the ease of always knowing exactly
what to say.
I'm just saying it was before I
grew angry,
grew out of my hometown,
grew acquainted with
my most dangerous questions
(we met like forbidden lovers
in the shadowy corner of myself),
grew hungry for something
more substantial for me to sink
my roots into.

Now,
I grow bravely,
grow daring enough to swallow
all the scripture that only
danced timid on the
tip of my tongue,
grow weary of the people who
are waiting to see when
my theology will become
bite-sized again;
waiting to see when I will
string it neat as pearls
across a single sentence.

I want to tell them about this
conviction that came and
found my prayers when they were
nothing but rage wrapped in barbed wire.

How it swells up waves
inside of me.

How, if I could part the flesh that
folds over my soul,
they would not find a still-water
reflection of themselves
but they would see Something
big enough to swallow
my life whole.

So, I set to
excavating it from myself.
I grow steam shovels for hands.
My fingers turn to pistons pressing
with mechanical precision
into all that was effortless
just moments ago.

I hope to come up with
earnestness shining on my hands,
but my palms only glimmer
with the shards of all the honesty
that I crushed under such
a forceful grasp.

And questions spout in smokestacks
from my mouth,
making a mockery of all that
has changed me.

"Aren't I holy?"

"Aren't you proud?"

"Aren't I (im)proving myself?"

* *"When I was a child, I spoke like a child, I thought like a child, I reasoned like a child. When I became a man, I gave up childish ways." -1 Corinthians 13:11, English Standard Version*

The Book of the Faith Healers

I have lost count of the times I
have seen my sister
swaddled angelically
in hospital sheets, but still smiling
with a Christmas-pageant trust that
outshines even
the most sterilized white.
IV tubes too often cling to her
like she's their salvation, and it's an
understandable mistake.

So it takes
all the grace I
can scrape from my smile
not to laugh
when a well-meaning woman asks
if I have thought to bring
a faith healer
into all her infirmity.
Asks if we have prayed--*really* prayed
for recovery.

This woman
who has never met my sister asks if she
is truly open
to the idea of divine healing.

As if my sister,
with her rose window eyes
could be any more cathedral than she
already is.

As if miracles always make it
to the people who are made
of pure hope.

God forgive me,
I'm not saying He wishes her
to walk through this world in a body that
crumbles
across more days than it doesn't.

I'm just wondering
how many of us
spend our lives forgetting
that for every Moses, there are
a million common men.

I'm just wondering how to tell
this woman that for every
"twelve apostles" there are temples
full of faithful
who are chosen to remain
right where they are.

I'm just wondering if, maybe,
I simply don't know how
to gather up the gall to ask for
the impossible, without feeling like I
am trying to corner
the Divine into my demands.

As if I ever could. He's never
been one to conform to my expectations.

133

Somewhere back between
a hell-bound anger and here,
His name became
a light in my throat
and the surprise of it all
warms the rest of me.

So, who am I to say
what shape He'll take next?

Maybe it'll be the impossible.

The Book of Joy

My God,
I was never any good
at being new.

I've always been the sort
of woman who is made of
second-hand psalms,
cast off was the polish of me
'til my skin wore into
something you could see through and I
gleamed like a blood-soaked smile,
forgetting that I
was never any good
at sifting the joy
from my mistakes,
at digging something more
than self-hatred
from the scuffs of me.

And this laugh
is a fresh life, laying me down
like a barely born infant
fresh from the belly of You.

The Book of How I Know I Believe in All This

I am changed, but not chin
held high as a fist in the air.

I am sure, but not shoulders
squared proud as a pedestal.

I am certain but not spine
about to break beneath all this
self-importance.

I am faith but not feet
rushing into every argument
they can find.

The Book of Bigger Than Me

I've spent almost a year
trying to dig a lifestyle out of Europe's
soil and I still feel, on my worst days,
like all the splendor of this place is trying
to spit my footprints back out of the
ground, so it can go back
to perfect smooth.

This is one of those countries
where the storms go on holiday.
The clouds lay themselves lazily
across the August sky
and wring the rain
from their hair and onto rooftops.

This is one of those summers
where the thunder casts itself
over the church bells like a spell.

This is one of those cathedrals
where my chest swells spire-high
with every sigh I take in,
as if I can walk away
with a piece of this place
lodged in my chest, if only I breathe
deeply enough.

Outside, the fragile foundation of a
medieval chapter house lays contently
across the grass.
It's set wide as
a troubadour's smile, lined with
stones like crone's teeth.

They say the story of this place
stole across almost twenty centuries to
find me here.

But I am from a concrete
fast lane of a country and this place
where I sit still seems
so storybook far away--like when
love comes to rest in your hands
after you have only learned
to recognize it from
some out-of-reach fairytale.

Still, I take it all in.
Or try to.
I see for myself if I can lay
my hands against all the time that
trembles in these walls, and I wish
for something as holy, as whole-hearted
as this place.

I want,
I try
to feel my faith
come alive in my fingers
'til I've got no choice
but to push
all the beauty it breaks open in me
out through my hands,
making something so majestic
it's big enough to play home
to every pilgrim that comes
to wrap them self in it.

So, God,
teach me the craft
of being a creator.
Help me make
a martyr of my ego.
May it die for something
bigger than a book-shaped dream.

ACKNOWLEDGEMENTS

I always put off typing out the acknowledgments for my books until the last possible moment, so it's no surprise I 've done this again. Here I am siphoning an iced chai latte (I should know by now that these do precious little to calm me down in instances like this.) and dreading the task at hand. Absolutely dreading it.

There are two reasons for said dread: One, I hate the feeling that I am forgetting someone--and I *always* feel like I'm forgetting someone, no matter how many drafts I write. Two, it always feels so pidley. So not enough. I start to think of all the years of support and help I have gotten to get where I am, and a line in the back portion of a book hardly seems enough. I hope everyone featured in here feels just how grateful I am. I hope I make that apparent to you on a consistent basis. If I don't, well, here's a segment in the back portion of a book to remind you.

I have so many people to thank for this book coming into fruition. First and foremost, you, reader. Thank you for investing your time in my work, for coming on this journey with me-- especially if you don't identify with this faith. I believe two things people don't hear Christians say nearly enough are "I'm sorry" and "Me, too." I hope with all my heart that you found both in this book.

A HUGE thank you to my fabulous Kickstarter donors (in no particular order):

-Chris Slaney (and Elise)
-Daniel Matas
-Jasmine Walsh
-Alysha Stout
-Trilby Sauer
-Jamee Hawn
-Rusti Lang
-Sabrina Atkins
-Sarah Simpson
-KellyAnn De Moll
-Laura Simpson
-Molly Hoy
-Amanda Marcus
-Lisa Di Mattéo
-Jennifer Ingram
-Melissa Jennings
-Zoe Jones
-Bridget Kelley-Lossada
-Katherine Cassidy
-Ashly Kim
-Edel Fitzpatrick
-Michala Rolle
-Leslie Shaw
-Gaia Grazi
-Bethany Wearden

-Robert Swaney
-Lauren Yaro
-Melanie Dosen
-Lindsey Pomputis
-Sean Townsend
-Holly Wright

You lovely souls placed your trust, and your hard-earned dollars into this project, with only some Instagram posts and a small video to go by. I've got no words for how over-the-moon that makes me feel. This book has been a work in progress for over two years now, and I am so grateful to you all for helping it claw its way out of me in its best possible form. Thank you, thank you, thank you! You are the sort of readers that authors dream of having.

Marya Layth and Will Bortz, thank you for your incredibly kind words, and for taking the time to read this book in the midst of your crazy writer schedules. It was such an honor to get endorsements from both of you poetic powerhouses.

Charity Samoulides, your editing skills astound me. Thank you for getting so excited about this project, for seeing exactly where I wanted to go, and for guiding me there so expertly. Your insight was truly invaluable.

To my parents, for their genuine, honest and unwavering dedication to this faith.

To my sister, a truly incredible confidant and a consistent example of strength.

To my brother, for occasionally kidnapping me and making me talk about "how I'm really doing."

To the church communities in Los Angeles, Ecclesia and Radius, and the women of Faith Played Out, who are perpetually setting an example of authentic, wholehearted living.

To Robert, who can personally attest to the fact that this poetry collection was the hardest and most harrowing to write. Thank you for daring to marry a writer, for telling me how much this book needed to be written when I thought otherwise, and for writing copy for it when I really didn't want to. You are a gentleman, a scholar and an utter dream. I'm so glad you're my person.

And lastly, to every one of you with whom I have had a moment of profound realness. You know who you are. Maybe we were relaxing on a living room couch with some wine. Or laying on a patch of grass and staring at the stars. Or sitting on a kitchen floor. Or hanging out in some establishment's parking lot WAY after they closed and kicked us out. Maybe it was none of those places, but the moments all had something in common: a tense kind of magic, a hesitation as whatever we were about to say quivered in our throat, and then a moment of relief as we watched whatever truth was said hover in the air between us and knew that the other wasn't going anywhere. I am so lucky to have you and these moments in my life. I love that we can hand our shadowy, messy parts over to each other and come out loving one another even deeper. This poetry is possible because you were such shining examples of acceptance through the years.

Thank you, all of you.

All my love,

Morgan

ABOUT THE AUTHOR

Morgan Nikola-Wren began writing poetry for
various literary periodicals in 2013. She is a
winner of the Pangaea Worldwide Poetry Slam,
2016, and has published three books of poetry.
Her debut book, Magic with Skin On, received
a Goodreads Choice nomination for Best Poetry
Book of 2017.

Morgan is perpetually searching for new
favorite words, more black clothing, and the
perfect design for her next tattoo. She ran away
to Germany with her husband's circus for a
year, but now works in Pasadena as a children's
librarian, which is not all that different when
you think about it.

If you enjoyed this book, please consider
supporting her by leaving a review on
Amazon.com.